James

Back to the Bible Study Guides

Judges: Ordinary People, Extraordinary God

Proverbs: The Pursuit of God's Wisdom

John: Face-to-Face with Jesus

Ephesians: Life in God's Family

Revelation: The Glorified Christ

JAMES

LIVING YOUR FAITH

WOODROW KROLL

CROSSWAY BOOKS

A PUBLISHING MINISTRY OF
GOOD NEWS PUBLISHERS
WHEATON, ILLINOIS

James: Living Your Faith

Published by Crossway Books
a publishing ministry of Good News Publishers
1300 Crescent Street
Wheaton, Illinois 60187

Cover design: Josh Dennis

Cover photo: iStock

First printing, 2007

Printed in the United States of America

ISBN 13: 978-1-58134-882-8
ISBN 10: 1-58134-882-7

Produced with the assistance of The Livingstone Corporation (www.LivingstoneCorp.com).

Project Staff: Neil Wilson

CH 17 16 15 14 13 12 11 10 09 08 07
15 14 13 12 11 10 9 8 7 6 5 4 3 2 1

Table of Contents

How to Use This Study

Your study of James will have maximum impact if you prayerfully read each day's Scripture passage. The entire text of the Book of James from the English Standard Version is included in the study, with the selected passages printed before each lesson's reading, so that everything you need is in one place. While we recommend reading the Scripture passage before you read the devotional, some have found it helpful to use the devotional as preparation for reading the Scripture. If you are unfamiliar with the English Standard Version (on which this series of studies is based), you might consider reading the devotional, followed by reading the passage again from a different Bible version. This will give you an excellent basis for considering the rest of the lesson.

After each devotional there are three sections designed to help you better understand and apply the lesson's Scripture passage.

Consider It—Several questions will help you unpack and reflect on the Scripture passage. These could be used for a small group discussion.

Express It—Suggestions for turning the insights from the lesson into prayer.

Go Deeper—The nature of this study makes it important to see the Book of James in the context of other passages and insights from Scripture. This brief section will allow you to consider some of the implications of the day's passage for the central theme of the study (Living Your Faith) as well as the way it fits with the rest of Scripture.

Lesson 1

Into the Frying Pan

Jesus had a very practical half brother. His name was James. James took a long time to recognize the true identity of his older sibling Jesus. But when he did, James became a highly effective communicator of how following Jesus applies to life where we live it!

James 1:1–18

Greeting

1 James, a servant of God and of the Lord
Jesus Christ,

To the twelve tribes in the Dispersion:

Greetings.

> ## *Key Verse*
>
> *Count it all joy, my brothers, when you meet trials of various kinds* (James 1:2).

Testing of Your Faith

2Count it all joy, my brothers, when you
meet trials of various kinds, 3for you know
that the testing of your faith produces
steadfastness. 4And let steadfastness have
its full effect, that you may be perfect and
complete, lacking in nothing.

5If any of you lacks wisdom, let him ask
God, who gives generously to all without
reproach, and it will be given him. 6But let
him ask in faith, with no doubting, for the
one who doubts is like a wave of the sea
that is driven and tossed by the wind. 7For
that person must not suppose that he will
receive anything from the Lord; 8he is a
double-minded man, unstable in all his
ways.

9Let the lowly brother boast in his exaltation, 10and the rich in his humiliation, because like a flower of the grass he will pass
away. 11For the sun rises with its scorching
heat and withers the grass; its flower falls,
and its beauty perishes. So also will the
rich man fade away in the midst of his
pursuits.

12Blessed is the man who remains steadfast under trial, for when he has stood the
test he will receive the crown of life, which
God has promised to those who love him.
13Let no one say when he is tempted, "I am
being tempted by God," for God cannot be
tempted with evil, and he himself tempts
no one. 14But each person is tempted
when he is lured and enticed by his own
desire. 15Then desire when it has con-
ceived gives birth to sin, and sin when it is
fully grown brings forth death.

16Do not be deceived, my beloved brothers. 17Every good gift and every perfect gift
is from above, coming down from the Father of lights with whom there is no varia-
tion or shadow due to change.18Of his own
will he brought us forth by the word of
truth, that we should be a kind of firstfruits
of his creatures.

Go Deeper

When the Bible speaks about wisdom, it always describes a joyful way of living. The Book of Proverbs in the Old Testament could be subtitled, "How to grow a joyful life." True wisdom never stops with what we know but can be seen in how we live. The litmus test for godly wisdom is joy. Godly wisdom comes from two sources—from God's Word and as a direct answer to prayer. Often, God supplies wisdom by reminding us of what He said in His Word.

(continued)

Go Deeper Continued ...

After James's description of the benefits of facing trials with joy, he immediately tells us how to get the joy we will need in order to face our troubles. Joy will come from the wisdom that comes from God. Both Paul (Rom. 5:1–5, Phil. 4:4–9) and Peter (1 Pet. 1:3–7) describe a wise way of living that produces joy. And James will return to this subject of godly wisdom later in this letter (James 3:13–18). Joy, we will discover, is the key to living our faith before a watching world.

When it comes to possible trials, tests and temptations in our future, we'd rather hear "if" than "when." We don't relish difficulty. In fact, we often pray that God will keep us from trouble rather than expecting Him to do what He promised—to be with us in trouble.

James was too wise to let us kid ourselves. He began his letter by dropping his readers (us) right into the frying pan. "When you meet trials" not, "If you meet trials." It sounds very much like James was picking up where his older half brother left off. One of the last promises Jesus made has this same frying-pan kind of tone: "In the world you will have tribulation. But take heart; I have overcome the world" (John 16:33). Jesus guaranteed "tribulation," and James taught us to expect "trials of various kinds." With a forecast like that, we ought to prepare for bad weather!

Once we face the fact that there's trouble ahead, two questions usually come to mind. Why does God allow these troubles, and how can we wisely handle trouble? James answers both questions. In fact, just before dropping us into the frying pan, he gives us a heatproof, flameproof covering that can keep us cool no matter how high the heat gets turned up. That covering is made of joy. "Count it all joy" summarizes a supernatural way to deal with trouble. "Count it all joy" is a powerful way to describe what it means to live our faith.

Part of the difficulty we have in reading "joy" and "trouble" in the same sentence has to do with our poor understanding of joy. We usually think of joy as primarily a "good feelings" word, but joy isn't measured by feelings. If we make joy a synonym of happiness, we've reduced joy to something we can hardly count on during troubles.

The first thing troubles destroy is happiness. Joy, however, can be sharpened by trouble. Note how Jesus lived this out when He faced the greatest "trouble" in His life—the cross: "Looking to Jesus, the founder and perfecter of our faith, who for the joy that was set before him endured the cross, despising the shame, and is seated at the right hand of the throne of God. Consider him who endured from sinners such hostility against himself, so that you may not grow weary or fainthearted" (Heb. 12:2–3).

Joy is endurance with a knowing smile. Joy sees the bigger picture, while happiness is blind. Happiness depends on what happens; joy remains no matter what happens. Happiness is an unstable and unpredictable feeling; joy flows from truthful faith.

The basis for joy as James describes it is knowing why troubles come. Troubles come to "test" faith. The tests that troubles create aren't supposed to make faith fail but to make faith stronger. This process takes us through steps of growth: "steadfastness," "perfect(ion)," "complete(ness)" and "lacking in nothing." (See James 1:4.)

"Steadfastness" is another word for endurance and patience. Troubles are the speed bumps on the road of life. They may slow us down, but they shouldn't prevent us from going on about our lives. If we go on, we will experience growth in other areas. "Perfect" translates the Greek word *teleios,* which means "something that has come to its end." When something or someone has fulfilled their design or purpose, they are *teleios* or "complete." God brings tests into our lives to make us *teleios,* to fulfill His design and purpose for us and to make us mature in Christ.

"Complete" refers to the way God works on us in every way. No area or part of us gets overlooked. And "lacking in nothing" confirms the fact that God, partly through testing, supplies us

"Anyone can claim faith as long as life is easy, but the evidence of genuine faith is seen when troubles come."

with everything we will need for this life and for eternity. God loves us deeply and allows tests and trials into our lives because He knows they are the best opportunity we have to learn to live our faith. Anyone can claim faith as long as life is easy, but the evidence of genuine faith is seen when troubles come. And they will.

Most of us are familiar with the Emergency Broadcast System that has been in place for half a century in the United States. We recognize the tone on the radio followed by the well-worn announcement, "This is a test; it is only a test ..." That's a good way to think about troubles in our lives. They are only tests of something good God wants to build in us—faith. If we can remember that fact, it will give us a reason for joy the next time we find ourselves in the frying pan of life.

Express It

There's nothing like a visit to the frying pan to provoke our prayers for wisdom! We may agree that facing trouble with joy is the wise way to live, but the reality of troubles reminds us how easy it is to forget about joy and get overwhelmed by our troubles. Often it isn't even the big troubles but the little ones that "give us real trouble." If you want to "count it all joy," you'll have to learn to ask for wisdom.

Consider It

As you read James 1:1–18, consider these questions:

1) **How does James compare faithful prayer and doubtful prayer in this chapter?**

2) **What is the ultimate result for the person who has remained steadfast through all the trials of life (v. 12)?**

3) **In what ways do both the rich and the poor benefit under God's blessing?**

4) **How are temptations different from trials?**

5) **What did you learn about God from these first 18 verses?**

6) **When has God answered your prayers for wisdom? What happened?**

7) **Describe one "trial" you are counting as joy in your life right now.**

Lesson 2

Mirror, Mirror

Even a flawless mirror can only give us a reversed image of ourselves. And mirrors are notoriously forgetful. They don't remember what we looked like yesterday. Then again, we don't remember what we looked like either. But what if we could look into a mirror that "knew" us, told us about ourselves and gave us direction?

James 1:19–27

Hearing and Doing the Word

19Know this, my beloved brothers: let every
person be quick to hear, slow to speak,
slow to anger; 20for the anger of man does
not produce the righteousness that God requires. 21Therefore put away all filthiness
and rampant wickedness and receive with
meekness the implanted word, which is
able to save your souls.

22But be doers of the word, and not hear-
ers only, deceiving yourselves. 23For if anyone is a hearer of the word and not a doer,
he is like a man who looks intently at his
natural face in a mirror. 24For he looks at
himself and goes away and at once forgets
what he was like. 25But the one who looks
into the perfect law, the law of liberty, and
perseveres, being no hearer who forgets
but a doer who acts, he will be blessed in
his doing.

26If anyone thinks he is religious and does
not bridle his tongue but deceives his
heart, this person's religion is worthless.
27Religion that is pure and undefiled before God, the Father, is this: to visit orphans and widows in their affliction, and
to keep oneself unstained from the world.

Key Verse

But the one who looks into the perfect law, the law of liberty, and perseveres, being no hearer who forgets but a doer who acts, he will be blessed in his doing (James 1:25).

Go Deeper

One of the byproducts of developing quicker hearing involves slower responses of anger. This doesn't mean that anger is never an appropriate response. Ephesians 4:26 reminds us, "Be angry and do not sin; do not let the sun go down on your anger." The issue quickly becomes not denying anger but learning to control it.

Other Scripture passages underscore the importance of slowing anger response time. Solomon noted in Proverbs, "A man of quick temper acts foolishly, and a man of evil devices is hated" (14:17), and "Whoever is slow to anger is better than the mighty, and he who rules his spirit than he who takes a city" (16:32). The warning comes in James 1:20, "for the anger of man does not produce the righteousness that God requires." The quicker the anger, the more likely it is merely a human expression. But anger that echoes God's anger over sin, anger under control, will be anger that acts wisely and does not sin.

Honest feedback can be very useful. It can confirm we're on the right track or steer us back in the right direction if we aren't. It may even prevent us from making a train wreck of our lives. So, why do we avoid or ignore feedback? Because, like trains, we find it hard to slow down or turn around. We're one-track-minded people who don't like to be told we might be going the wrong way, even if the feedback is meant for our good.

God's Word fits into a special category of feedback. In fact, the Bible gives us as much "feed-forward" (instructions into the future) as feedback. When God speaks, we ought to reconsider any thought we have about getting a second opinion. In this lesson's key verse, James summarized the compelling reasons why we should be attentive to God's Word and active in carrying out His instructions. The approach produces a life marked by balance and blessing.

James has already warned us in this chapter that a life spent ignoring or blaming God has a predictable result: death (James 1:15). Everyone faces trials and temptations. What distinguishes the godly from the ungodly is the way we respond to them. Do we live by our wits or by God's Word? Our wits suggest that temptations are God's fault; God's Word holds up the truth mirror and shows us how our desires derail us (1:13–16). Our wits lead us to listen slowly, speak too quickly and leap to angry conclusions. God's Word contradicts our instincts, telling us to "be quick to hear, slow to speak, slow to anger" (1:19).

Isn't it interesting that God gave us two ears, two hands, two eyes, but only one mouth? All of these points of contact with the world need to be under control, but our speech needs added attention. Silence is undervalued. Abraham Lincoln explained part of the value of silence when he commented, "Better to remain silent and be thought a fool, than to open your mouth and remove all doubt."

So, what does James mean by "quick to hear?" Verse 21 gives us two clues—"put away" and "receive with meekness." We have to eliminate the distractions of "filthiness and wickedness" and develop an eager receptivity to God's Word. The little phrase "quick to hear" challenges the way we approach God's Word. Casual and occasional attention to what God says will probably not yield the results in our lives that God intends.

But James isn't finished with us. We might conclude that "hearing" is simply "taking in" and perhaps "remembering." That conclusion, says James, would be "deceiving yourselves." Hearing isn't complete until we've put what we heard into action. Hearing comes before doing, but hearing by itself is an unacceptable approach to God's Word. It's treating God's Word like we treat mirrors, quickly forgetting what we see in them. James wants us never to set down God's Word without asking, "Lord, what should I do as a result of what I have just heard You say to me?"

James also calls God's Word, "the perfect law, the law of liberty" (v. 25). We're not used to seeing "law" and "liberty" in the same sentence except as opposites. We often assume that the degree of freedom is in direct inverse proportion to the degree of law. But God's perfect law actually prevents freedom from becoming another form of slavery.

When we apply the world's (our wit's) definition of freedom—doing whatever we desire—we quickly end up in bondage to bad decisions. But God's Word demonstrates wisdom by directing our choices and keeping us free. Real freedom isn't doing whatever we desire; real freedom is doing what God desires. That's the purpose behind our creation.

So, while our wits want to give our tongues free rein, God's Word applies a bridle (v. 26). Our wits tell us to associate with people like ourselves and make personal entertainment our highest priority. But God's Word gives us truthful feedback. If we want to give God pleasure and enjoy His blessings, then we must associate with "orphans and widows in their affliction, and to keep oneself unstained from the world" (v. 27).

When Jesus was asked to define a neighbor, He illustrated His answer with a story about two people, a person in need and an unexpected helper. (See Luke 10:30–37.) If you want to be a

> *"Real freedom isn't doing whatever we desire; real freedom is doing what God desires. That's the purpose behind our creation."*

good neighbor, surprise someone in need by helping him or her. Ask God to help you notice "afflicted" people in your life and then to give you wisdom in how to best help them.

We can all improve our speed when it comes to listening more quickly. God's Word assures us that as we act, we will experience God's blessing. Note the last phrase in the key verse: "he will be blessed in his doing." Keep looking in the mirror of God's Word, and keep doing all it asks of you.

Express It

Make a short list of the people you know who are presently experiencing "affliction." Pray for them, asking God to give you clear direction on what you might do to visit them with practical help. Then make sure you visit at least one of those people this week.

Consider It

As you read James 1:19–27, consider these questions:

1) **How are speaking, hearing and anger connected in this passage?**

2) **What are the upsides and the downsides of anger?**

3) **What prevents us from hearing God's Word the right way?**

4) **When have you found freedom in the law?**

5) **Why is "doing" the last step of "hearing"?**

6) **How do you keep yourself "unstained from the world"?**

Lesson 3

Playing Favorites

Celebrities expect special treatment. The lunch line rules don't apply to them, whether they're in a cafeteria or on a nationally televised event. Certain people assume they will receive preferential treatment. Where did they get that idea? Why does someone come to think that they're exempt from waiting, poor seats and the leftovers? Perhaps it's because we train them to think that way.

James 2:1–13

The Sin of Partiality

2 My brothers, show no partiality as you
hold the faith in our Lord Jesus Christ, the
Lord of glory. [2]For if a man wearing a gold
ring and fine clothing comes into your as-
sembly, and a poor man in shabby clothing also comes in, [3]and if you pay attention to the one who wears the fine clothing
and say, "You sit here in a good place,"
while you say to the poor man, "You stand
over there," or, "Sit down at my feet,"
[4]have you not then made distinctions
among yourselves and become judges with
evil thoughts? [5]Listen, my beloved brothers, has not God chosen those who are
poor in the world to be rich in faith and
heirs of the kingdom, which he has promised to those who love him? [6]But you have
dishonored the poor man. Are not the rich
the ones who oppress you, and the ones
who drag you into court? [7]Are they not the
ones who blaspheme the honorable name
by which you were called?

Key Verse

If you really fulfill the royal law according to the Scripture, "You shall love your neighbor as yourself," you are doing well (James 2:8).

[8]If you really fulfill the royal law according
to the Scripture, "You shall love your
neighbor as yourself," you are doing well.
[9]But if you show partiality, you are commit-
ting sin and are convicted by the law as
transgressors. [10]For whoever keeps the
whole law but fails in one point has become accountable for all of it. [11]For he who
said, "Do not commit adultery," also said,
"Do not murder." If you do not commit
adultery but do murder, you have become
a transgressor of the law. [12]So speak and
so act as those who are to be judged under the law of liberty. [13]For judgment is
without mercy to one who has shown no
mercy. Mercy triumphs over judgment.

Go Deeper

Since the next lesson will focus on the subject of faith, it's worth noting that James has already offered several significant insights about faith up to this point in his letter. We already learned that faith is tested (James 1:3) by various kinds of trials. Prayer must be presented "in faith" (1:6), expecting God to provide wisdom. Faith is "in our Lord Jesus Christ, the Lord of glory," and we must "hold" it consistently in the way we treat others (2:1).

God chooses people who are "poor in the world to be rich in faith," possibly because they are less likely than the rich to rely on their possessions for security (v. 5). Although James uses the term "religion" instead of "faith" in James 1:26–27, he's actually making the point that faith isn't just about "religious" claims and actions. Faith actions boil down to loving God and loving our neighbor in this messy world.

Jesus made it clear on numerous occasions (see John 13–17) that those who claim to love Him must obey His commands. Loving God can't be reduced to warm feelings toward Him. Loving God has to do with the way we relate to those around us under His guidance. That's faith in action.

Times may change, but certain social characteristics remain. Jesus was right—the poor are always with us. Almost any effort to be faithful to Jesus' teaching will involve a growing awareness of the needs of people around us.

The poor come in many forms, and their poverty is not always measured by lack of money. In almost any human situation, some will have more and some will have less. James has indicated that even this is part of God's plan. In James 1:9–10 he wrote, "Let the lowly brother boast in his exaltation, and the rich in his humiliation, because like a flower of the grass he will pass away."

The part of the Bible that James was most familiar with was what we call the Old Testament, and it is filled with passages that talk about God's gift of riches to us. Jesus' half brother echoes much of the wisdom Solomon recorded in places like Ecclesiastes 5:19: "Everyone also to whom God has given wealth and possessions and power to enjoy them, and to accept his lot and rejoice in his toil—this is the gift of God."

Both work and contentment are God's gifts. Jobs, energy and opportunity are means by which wealth arrives, but the ultimate giver of wealth is always God the Father. When a rich person recognizes that his possessions are part of God's gift to him, the moment can be a very humbling experience. The "boasting" James encourages in regard to the rich and poor has to do with our relationship with God no matter what our status in the world.

Jeremiah wrote one of the classic statements of the contrast between what we think is worth boasting about and what God thinks is worthy of boasting. "Thus says the Lord: 'Let not the wise man boast in his wisdom, let not the mighty man boast in his might, let not the rich man boast in his riches, but let him who boasts boast in this, that he understands and knows me, that I am the Lord who practices steadfast love, justice, and righteousness in the earth. For in these things I delight, declares the Lord" (Jer. 9:23–24).

Knowing God is both the greatest claim and the most humbling relationship a person can have. Among followers of Jesus, genuine fellowship between the rich and the poor begins with the rich understanding that they are not better than the poor simply because they are wealthy. Every lot in life can be an opportunity to learn and practice humility. Humble feelings are illusive, but there are always humble tasks that can be performed.

For example, tell your church janitor that the next time he goes on vacation, you'd like to volunteer to clean the bathrooms while he's gone. Or stay behind after the worship service next week, walk to the front of the sanctuary, and then make your way back through the pews/chairs, picking up the "left behinds" like bulletins, wrappers and miscellaneous trash.

The first section of James 2 continues the concerns of the first chapter. Not only were the believers missing opportunities to help orphans and widows, they were also showing preference for the wealthy. They were in danger of falling for the lure of influence rather than recognizing the power of integrity. James reminded them of the value of the poor and the difficulties often created by the rich. After all, the poor were not likely to oppress, wield the law or mock Christ. But the biggest reason for not practicing partiality had to do with the "royal law according to Scripture, 'You shall love your neighbor as yourself'" (James 2:8).

Those to whom James was writing were most likely poor themselves. James was reminding them of the command to treat all others as we want to be treated. The point wasn't to honor the poor and treat the wealthy with disrespect but to treat everyone with honor and respect. He wanted believers to be known as groups where all were welcomed, whatever their status.

This approach, of course, violates the rule of the pecking order. It puts the rich and famous among regular folk. It practices the biblical belief that every person in the body of Christ has been given a gift that the rest of the body needs. People usually need to feel welcomed and valued before they feel free to exercise their spiritual gifts. But if the warmth of our welcome has to

"Every lot in life can be an opportunity to learn and practice humility. Humble feelings are illusive, but there are always humble tasks that can be performed."

do with social status, James says we are violating a command of God that is just as crucial as His commands about adultery or murder (2:9–11).

James says we ought to treat each other with "mercy." It's not our place to decide what treatment people deserve. We're supposed to be so aware of the way God continually exercises mercy toward us that we actually look for opportunities to exercise it with others whether they deserve it or not. When we are not merciful, we demonstrate how little we understand and appreciate the mercy we have received. We don't treat others with respect and honor because of what we expect them to do for us, because they deserve it or because they have earned it, but because we have been humbled by God's mercy toward us sinners.

Express It

As you pray about partiality, ask God to show you ways you are prone to treat others based on what you think they might do for you rather than based on mercy. Describe to God how you understand and appreciate His present mercy toward you. If necessary, write out a list of evidences of His mercy in your life. Let that awareness affect the way you pray for and treat others.

Consider It

As you read James 2:1–13, consider these questions:

1) **What does our partiality say to God?**

That we think we can judge others. That I don't see or understand my own need for a Savior + His mercy.

2) **How has God honored the "poor in the world" (v. 5)?**

He has given them a grace to be rich in faith + the promise to be heirs of His Kingdom.

3) **In what ways does a person's outward appearance affect you?**

Extra visual attention, maybe stereotype Feel compassion, want to help/give

4) **What does an impartial welcome in the church look like?**

No difference in how we greet or welcome or invite

5) **How would you illustrate the command to "love your neighbor as yourself" (v. 8)?**

For me it's an open heart + home + willingness to help/give just like they're family.

6) **What have other Christians done for you to make you feel welcome or accepted?**

warm greeting, hug, invite into home or out to lunch/dinner, not judged, prayed for

7) **Name some specific "humble jobs" that might need doing in your church that you could do. Which ones will you do? When will you do them?**

trash out, pick up after services/events, greet, pray, child care

Lesson 4

Faith That Works

People often try to apply a common-sense approach to heaven. They don't feel good enough to deserve heaven, and they don't think their faith is strong enough to get them there, so they come to a widely held conclusion: God must grade on the curve. He can't take in everybody, so He'll take in those who have done the most good. Could that be right? What matters most, faith or effort? And how much faith or effort is enough?

James 2:14–26

Faith Without Works Is Dead

14What good is it, my brothers, if someone says he has faith but does not have works? Can that faith save him? 15If a brother or sister is poorly clothed and lacking in daily food, 16and one of you says to them, "Go in peace, be warmed and filled," without giving them the things needed for the body, what good is that? 17So also faith by itself, if it does not have works, is dead.

Key Verse

What good is it, my brothers, if someone says he has faith but does not have works? Can that faith save him? (James 2:14).

18But someone will say, "You have faith and I have works." Show me your faith apart from your works, and I will show you my faith by my works. 19You believe that God is one; you do well. Even the demons believe—and shudder! 20Do you want to be shown, you foolish person, that faith apart from works is useless? 21Was not Abraham our father justified by works when he offered up his son Isaac on the altar? 22You see that faith was active along with his works, and faith was completed by his works; 23and the Scripture was fulfilled that says, "Abraham believed God, and it was counted to him as righteousness"—and he was called a friend of God. 24You see that a person is justified by works and not by faith alone. 25And in the same way was not also Rahab the prostitute justified by works when she received the messengers and sent them out by another way? 26For as the body apart from the spirit is dead, so also faith apart from works is dead.

Go Deeper

Abraham and Rahab fit at opposite ends of the social spectrum. One was the patriarch of Israel; the other was a Canaanite prostitute. One had an almost impeccable reputation; the other was a woman of "ill repute." But Abraham and Rahab actually had at least three significant traits in common: 1) both had their shortcomings; 2) both were in Jesus' family tree and 3) both were examples of living faith.

Abraham is mentioned throughout Scripture, but his life story is told in Genesis 11:27–25:11. Rahab plays her role in Bible history in Joshua 2:1–24; 6:22–25 and Matthew 1:5. Both lived less-than-perfect lives, and yet both are mentioned in the Hall of Faith in Hebrews 11. Both offer us a lot of hope about what God can do with our lives, wherever we find ourselves socially!

The apostle Paul (Rom. 4:1–5) may seem to disagree with James in assessing Abraham's life, but the two biblical writers were making complementary points. Paul pointed out the basis of Abraham's faith; James focused on the effects of Abraham's faith. Both men taught that faith in Christ was central and must affect all of life. Paul demolished "faith in works" while James demolished "faith without works." Both practiced and taught "faith that works." That's the kind of faith you want.

Teachers have known about the "bell curve" for a long time. In a typical classroom, if the students' grades are graphed, the below-average, average and above-average grades will create a bell or hill-shaped line. The largest group is average and the numbers of below-average and above-average students will form the slopes on either side. A grading system based on the curve means that a teacher decides on a magic point in the learning curve. Every grade below that point doesn't pass. Every grade above that point passes. In this picture, no one gets a perfect failure or success grade. Each person fits somewhere on the curve.

It's almost eerie how often people try to apply the bell curve to God's dealings with them. This kind of thinking even affects people who have spent a lot of time in church. They will agree that we can observe a variety of successes in living moral lives. Shown a bell curve on a sheet of paper, they can suggest names that should be placed on the right side of the curve, like Billy Graham and Mother Theresa. They will also mention names that fit on the left side, like Hitler, Hussein and other notorious tyrants. If told that the passing grade is a point at the center of the curve and then asked to locate where their lives fit, they will almost invariably put themselves right next to the passing grade, on one side or the other. Asked if they know they have passed, many will shrug and admit their uncertainty. A few will confess they live lives of quiet desperation, not knowing from one day to the next if God would give their lives a passing grade. They need some good news! They are ready to hear about Christ.

One reason people fail to respond to Jesus Christ is because they have concluded that God grades lives on the curve, and they hope they're getting a passing grade. Some have even found a biblical basis for their approach in this passage in James. They are wrong. They are focusing on one of three kinds of faith, the very one James *doesn't* discuss in this passage. James does contrast "faith without works" and "faith that works." He ignores the third kind, "faith in works," because he knows that isn't genuine faith at all. But those who believe God grades on a curve are practicing faith in works. That's not faith in Christ; it's faith in their own efforts, and that's always bound to fail.

People who have a problem with James at this point are often reacting to things he *didn't* write. James didn't say faith and works are interchangeable. He definitely didn't claim that works replace or are better than faith. His focus in this passage is on those who are claiming a faith disconnected from life and those with a faith that connects with life.

James was concerned about the two ways people were living out their claims to faith in Christ. He made some crucial points. Pure belief doesn't have to influence behavior, but if it doesn't, it isn't worth much. His scathing comment, "You believe that God is one; you do well. Even the demons believe—and shudder!" (James 2:19), ought to make us shudder. James is "holding our feet to the fire" by insisting that if what we say we believe doesn't significantly affect the way we live, then what we actually believe is different from what we are saying. He illustrates this powerfully from Old Testament lives (see *Go Deeper*).

Let's return to the bell curve for a moment. Does it accurately picture human standing before God? Absolutely not. Both the Bible and observation produce the same devastating conclusion: "All have sinned and fall short of the glory of God" (Rom. 3:23). If human effort is graphed, no one can be considered "passing" because God demands perfection, and none of us can achieve it. God doesn't grade on the curve; He grades on pass/fail. All humanity fails. Compared to one another we may find degrees of moral difference; some may live lives that are more morally acceptable. But compared to God's standard, no one qualifies. Everyone fails.

For followers of Jesus, "works" aren't about gaining acceptance with God but always about expressing gratitude for acceptance from God. Faith in works is "so-that-God-might-save-me" living; genuine active faith in Christ is "because-God-has-saved-me" living. What we couldn't possibly earn, God gives freely by grace.

"God doesn't grade on the curve; He grades on pass/fail. Compared to one another we may find degrees of moral difference. But compared to God's standard, no one qualifies. Everyone fails."

If the overwhelming nature of God's gift doesn't change your life, you haven't understood (or perhaps even accepted) God's free gift of salvation yet. Since "faith in works" would require perfect performance, it's too late for any of us. Fortunately, the thankful living that faith in Christ requires is well within our reach. Think about it. How will your life today be a grateful expression for what you know Christ has done for you?

Express It

Ask God for harmony between your trust in Him and your obedience to Him. Put James's guidance into action, and seek God's wisdom in responding to life's challenges. Read James 2:15–17 again and pray about the way you tend to respond to people in need. How are your actions an expression of your faith?

Consider It

As you read James 2:14–26, consider these questions:

1) **How would you explain the relationship between faith and works?**

If my faith is real + true, then I will naturally have works in my life that are evidence of my real faith.

2) **What's the difference between dead faith and living faith?**

Dead - merely words or beliefs that don't affect daily living.
Living - active with natural evidence.

3) **What kind of "faith" do demons have?**

Merely belief that God is real + alive + powerful.

4) **Where, if anyplace, does James allude to "faith in works" as opposed to "faith without works" or "faith that works"?**

Not

5) **How does James use Abraham and Rahab to teach about living faith?**

By telling how their actions proved their faith was alive.

6) **How does James use the relationship of body and spirit to teach about faith and works?**

Like the body is dead w/o the spirit, so faith seems dead w/o evidence.

7) **In what ways does your faith work?**

serving, giving to needs, obedience to God

Lesson 5

Speech Control

To people overly concerned with what might pollute them, Jesus said, "Hear and understand: it is not what goes into the mouth that defiles a person, but what comes out of the mouth; this defiles a person" (Matt. 15:10–11). His half brother James echoed the same theme.

James 3:1–12

Taming the Tongue

3 Not many of you should become teachers, my brothers, for you know that we who teach will be judged with greater strictness. 2For we all stumble in many ways, and if anyone does not stumble in what he says, he is a perfect man, able also to bridle his whole body. 3If we put bits into the mouths of horses so that they obey us, we guide their whole bodies as well. 4Look at the ships also: though they are so large and are driven by strong winds, they are guided by a very small rudder wherever the will of the pilot directs. 5So also the tongue is a small member, yet it boasts of great things.

How great a forest is set ablaze by such a small fire! 6And the tongue is a fire, a world of unrighteousness. The tongue is set among our members, staining the whole body, setting on fire the entire course of life, and set on fire by hell. 7For every kind of beast and bird, of reptile and sea creature, can be tamed and has been tamed by mankind, 8but no human being can tame the tongue. It is a restless evil, full of deadly poison. 9With it we bless our Lord and Father, and with it we curse people who are made in the likeness of God. 10From the same mouth come blessing and cursing. My brothers, these things ought not to be so. 11Does a spring pour forth from the same opening both fresh and salt water? 12Can a fig tree, my brothers, bear olives, or a grapevine produce figs? Neither can a salt pond yield fresh water.

Key Verse

For we all stumble in many ways, and if anyone does not stumble in what he says, he is a perfect man, able also to bridle his whole body (James 3:2).

Go Deeper

The first half of this passage focuses on the effect the tongue has on its owner. The tongue causes stumbles (James 3:2), fires (3:5), stains (v. 6) and "a world of unrighteousness" (v. 6). But the tongue also creates damage to others, spreading poison (v. 8) and cursing "people who are made in the likeness of God" (v. 9).

Washington Irving observed, "A sharp tongue is the only edged tool that grows keener with constant use." Irving's keen insight proves true in both positive and negative ways. The more we use our tongues to slash and burn, the more skillful they become in that task. But the more we use our tongues to help and encourage others, the more able they become in that pursuit as well.

Remember the truth that "death and life are in the power of the tongue, and those who love it will eat its fruits" (Prov. 18:21). You can give life through your tongue. What you say can encourage the dejected. Your words can comfort the sorrowing. And through your

(continued)

Go Deeper Continued ...

mouth, others can hear words that describe the gift of eternal life and invite them to receive it.

When King David stopped lying to himself about a sequence of sins and repented before God, he knew what one of the benefits of forgiveness would be. He prayed, "Restore to me the joy of your salvation, and uphold me with a willing spirit. Then I will teach transgressors your ways, and sinners will return to you" (Ps. 51:12–13).

Little things can make a big difference. Small parts can have a huge effect. And tiny glitches can create huge disasters. James begins his third chapter with several illustrations that are, if possible, even more true today. His point about a rudder's effect on a wind-driven ship is magnified many times over if we think of an aircraft carrier or a passenger jet straying off course. James wanted his readers to understand what a significant role our tongues play in steering us into or out of trouble.

This lesson's key verse states the issue positively: tongue-control is usually evidence of general self-control. James almost has his tongue in cheek when he points out that the first place most of us stumble is when we trip over our own tongues.

Clydesdales are beautiful and massive horses. Harnessed to a plow or wagon, they can exert tremendous power. And yet, as James reminds us, even the most powerful horse can be steered with a small bit in its mouth.

And James didn't stop with the insight about the power of small things. He added the caution that small things can easily grow into large things, gradually developing strength. I have seen this illustrated in a location in Israel I have visited a number of times over the years. I can remember a certain sidewalk that was placed to facilitate visits to a historic location. When it was new, the poured concrete slabs appeared to be a permanent addition to the landscape. Several years later, I noticed a tiny seedling had taken root in one of the expansion joints of the sidewalk. Impressed with its tenacity, the custodial crew must have left the little tree alone. It grew. In the contest between tree and cement, something had to give. Imperceptibly, the root system and developing trunk of the tree exerted irresistible power. Huge slabs were shoved aside. Now the sidewalk goes around the tree. What was small and weak became large and strong.

The principle of patient power can be applied in both healthy and harmful ways in our lives. James tells us that our tongues can cause sparks (James 3:5–6). These might not be impressive in themselves, but if we produce them in a combustible atmosphere, a huge fire may develop.

Conversely, a small but relentless positive habit like daily Bible reading, or a consistent pattern of encouragement, can eventually produce amazing results. David the psalmist painted a beautiful word picture of patient power when he wrote, "Blessed is the man who walks not in the counsel of the wicked, nor stands in the way of sinners, nor sits in the seat of scoffers; but his delight is in the law of the LORD, and on his law he meditates day and night. He is like a tree planted by streams of water that yields its fruit in its season, and its leaf does not wither. In all that he does, he prospers" (Ps. 1:1–3). The transition from acorn to oak happens every day but too slowly for us to notice until the results become apparent.

Our tongues, James tells us, are in a special category. They are ultimately untamable. In other words, we may be able to develop speech control, but our tongues will always retain a wild streak. Our tongues will always be capable of contradiction—trying to say two opposite things at the same time. "My brothers," James pleads, "these things ought not to be so" (James 3:10).

Our tongues, like rudders and bridles, are instruments under the control of a will. A rudder doesn't decide on its own to steer the ship into the cliff, the one at the helm makes that decision. In a sobering way, our tongues reflect us. Our tongues put our thoughts into words. If our minds are full of sparks and evil intentions, they will escape through our speech. If our

> *"If we're at the helm and our tongues are the rudders that steer the ship of our lives, then who is the captain? Are we charting our own course or listening to the Captain's instructions?"*

hearts are divided in their love for God and others, our tongues will send mixed messages. Solomon tells us, "The heart of the wise makes his speech judicious and adds persuasiveness to his lips" (Prov. 16:23).

If we're at the helm and our tongues are the rudders that steer the ship of our lives, then who is the captain? Are we charting our own course or listening to the Captain's instructions? We are capable of doing so much damage through our words that we ought to be constantly seeking God's guidance. Those around us will be blessed as we develop speech control. Not only will they be spared the sharp and hurtful things we can so easily say, but they will also be blessed as we share the wisdom we learn from God.

Express It

King David ended one of his psalms with a perceptive prayer that you can use regularly for help in speech control: "Let the words of my mouth and the meditation of my heart be acceptable in your sight, O Lord, my rock and my redeemer" (Ps. 19:14).

Consider It

As you read James 3:1–12, consider these questions:

1) **How does the first verse in this chapter relate to what follows?**

Teachers use their words/tongues to influence positively, so they need to be very aware of their example with their tongue when not teaching.

2) **According to verse 2, why would it be impossible to call ourselves perfect?**

'Cuz no one has ever not done wrong with their words... everyone stumbles.

3) **How useful would a warning like, "When in doubt, pray rather than say," be to you?**

Very useful... it would change a lot that I say without thinking it through.

4) **Bit, rudder, spark, mixed messages, mixed waters and mixed fruit—which illustration tells you the most about your tongue?**

Spark

5) **When was the last time your words got you in trouble? What did you learn from that stumble?**

Sun. I need to encourage + complement way more than I joke + tease.

6) **How does this passage offer you specific help with speech control?**

It calls it out like it is, so I am aware of the power my words have. It uses truth + conviction to expose my need.

Wisdom's Sources

There are apparently two forms of wisdom operating in the world. The outward appearance of those who represent either wisdom does not reveal that they are wise or what form of wisdom they possess. Someone may look wise yet practice foolishness. Another may seem foolish by the world's standard and turn out to be exercising godly wisdom. How can we know the difference?

James 3:13–18

Wisdom from Above

[13]Who is wise and understanding among
you? By his good conduct let him show his
works in the meekness of wisdom. [14]But if
you have bitter jealousy and selfish ambition in your hearts, do not boast and be
false to the truth. [15]This is not the wisdom
that comes down from above, but is earthly, unspiritual, demonic. [16]For where jealousy and selfish ambition exist, there will
be disorder and every vile practice. [17]But
the wisdom from above is first pure, then
peaceable, gentle, open to reason, full of
mercy and good fruits, impartial and sincere. [18]And a harvest of righteousness is
sown in peace by those who make peace.

Key Verse

But the wisdom from above is first pure, then peaceable, gentle, open to reason, full of mercy and good fruits, impartial and sincere (James 3:17).

Go Deeper

This lesson's key verse offers an itemized list of eight traits of godly, wise living. "But the wisdom from above is first pure, then peaceable, gentle, open to reason, full of mercy and good fruits, impartial and sincere" (James 3:17). Note how strikingly similar this list is to the fruit of the Spirit: "But the fruit of the Spirit is love, joy, peace, patience, kindness, goodness, faithfulness, gentleness, self-control; against such things there is no law" (Gal. 5:22–23).

Godly, wise living is life in the Spirit, a journey that begins when we turn our lives over to Christ and receive His life in exchange for ours. Along with the gift of eternal life comes the gift of the indwelling Holy Spirit. (See John 3:6; Rom. 8:1–2; Eph. 1:13–14.)

Both Paul (Gal. 5:24) and James (3:14–16) point out the barriers that must be removed as we seek to live by godly wisdom. As Paul puts it, we must crucify "the flesh with its passions and desires." Doesn't that sound like James's "bitter jealousy and selfish ambition"? These insights help you understand what Jesus meant when He said, "If anyone would come after me, let him deny himself and take up his cross and follow me" (Matt. 16:24).

Godly wisdom and faith must be siblings. They come from the same source. Their presence is felt in the same way—by the actions they produce. James had just finished a section in which he described the way we tend to want to talk out of both sides of our mouths. Now he shifts to the issue of wisdom. We can't have it both ways, he writes. We can't be giving mixed messages to the world. Progress in godly wisdom will yield good conduct (James 3:13) and integrity of character (3:17).

James describes two kinds of wisdom operating in the world. Before looking at the differences, it would be good to have a working definition of wisdom. A wise person has a clear world-view, a specific way of looking at life. A wise person applies this worldview to his or her way of life. In other words, wisdom is applied truth. The closer wisdom's worldview parallels reality, the closer it comes to pure, godly wisdom. James calls this wisdom "from above" (v. 15). The farther wisdom ignores reality, the farther it moves from the truth. James calls this "earthly, unspiritual, demonic" (v. 15) wisdom.

So, why are these opposite ends of the worldview spectrum both called "wisdom"? Can someone be wisely evil? All wisdom shares at least one significant trait: practicality. Both earthly and heavenly wisdom are about getting things done. Jesus said, "For the sons of this world are more shrewd in dealing with their own generation than the sons of light" (Luke 16:8).

The word "shrewd" can be translated "wise" in that verse. But how could people who don't know God be more practical, shrewd and "wise" than people who know God? Because sometimes the path we take looks right and seems right until we come around the final turn and realize we're on the wrong side of the canyon. Because "there is a way that seems right to a man, but its end is the way to death" (Prov. 14:12). It's a painful truth that we can live a wise life and end up at the wrong destination.

God has built patterns and structures into the universe that can be used wisely by people whether or not they acknowledge God. A wicked farmer may have as good a harvest as a godly one if both are following agricultural practices in harmony with God's creation. Two non-Christians may have a better marriage than two Christians if the former have learned and applied God's principles for relationships (even if they don't realize the source). A craftsman in any field has learned the "wisdom" related to that field that God originally designed.

But when it comes to the big picture and the purpose of life, people move from general wisdom in two directions: earthly and godly. James points out that earthly wisdom is driven by "jealousy and selfish ambition" (James 3:14,16). People can strive for high standards and excellence for the wrong reasons. Earthly, unspiritual and demonic wisdom is self-seeking (3:15). People may be very effective in their pursuits for entirely selfish reasons, which turn out to be dead ends. The more a society is practicing little besides earthly wisdom, the more it will be characterized by "disorder and every vile practice" (v. 16).

History is full of groups or movements that have risen based on applied principles of wisdom in warfare and government but have eventually collapsed and failed because the byproducts (disorder and vile practices) overwhelmed the wise structures that allowed them to flourish. Earthly wisdom does lead to achievement but ultimately at too high a cost. Jesus was talking about earthly wisdom when He asked, "For what will it profit a man if he gains the whole world and forfeits his life? Or what shall a man give in return for his life?" (Matt. 16:26).

Godly wisdom, says James, produces "a harvest of righteousness [that] is sown in peace" (James 3:18). He points out eight characteristics that will be present in situations where godly wisdom is used. Such wisdom is "first pure, then peaceable, gentle, open to reason, full of mercy and good fruits, impartial and sincere" (3:17).

"Earthly wisdom does lead to achievement but ultimately at too high a cost."

Godly wisdom is available but too seldom accessed by those who have every reason to want their lives to exhibit that kind of wisdom. James tells us we can't be wise unless we are ready to live wisely. And we can't live wisely unless we are continuously seeking to conform our lives to the One who is Wisdom. Living wisely comes down to learning to live under God's commands.

Express It

The "meekness of wisdom" is godly power that doesn't show off or boast (James 3:13). We don't ask God for His wisdom so that we can impress others. We ask Him for wisdom because we know He is the ultimate source. We ask Him for wisdom because we understand how quickly we reach the end of our wisdom (1:5). The qualities of godly wisdom (3:17) are only found in places where God has been asked to work and has been given freedom to do His work in peoples' lives. Ask God to pour His wisdom into your life for His purposes.

Consider It

As you read James 3:13–18, consider these questions:

1) **How do verses 13–18 apply and drive home the lessons in verses 1–12?**

Wisdom is applied truth + will affect how we speak + the things we say.

2) **Who are some people you know who are wise in earthly wisdom?**

boss, PF,

3) **What are some examples of other good results from earthly wisdom?**

4) **Who are some people you know who are wise in godly wisdom?**

PF, Mike, my homies

5) **How does verse 14 offer guidelines for examining our motives?**

Shouldn't be boasting about anything except God.

6) **What does James mean by "bitter jealousy" and "selfish ambition" in verses 14 and 16?**

Envying others for what they have + wondering why I don't have it.

7) **After reading *Go Deeper*, what are some of the practices you want to emphasize in your life that promote godly wisdom?**

Lead my family by ex. with my speech + reactions. Crucify my own will + live a life of servanthood.

8) **How would you describe a "harvest of righteousness" (v. 18)?**

Like the law of sowing + reaping. Right char. before God + right actions before men.

Escape from Worldliness

Jesus leveled with us when He said, "I am no longer in the world, but they are in the world. . . . I do not ask that you take them out of the world, but that you keep them from the evil one" (John 17:11,15). If we have to live in the world, what practical life decisions can we make to keep us from becoming of *the world?*

James 4:1–12

Warning Against Worldliness

4 What causes quarrels and what causes fights among you? Is it not this, that your passions are at war within you? 2You desire and do not have, so you murder. You covet and cannot obtain, so you fight and quarrel. You do not have, because you do not ask. 3You ask and do not receive, because you ask wrongly, to spend it on your passions. 4You adulterous people! Do you not know that friendship with the world is enmity with God? Therefore whoever wishes to be a friend of the world makes himself an enemy of God. 5Or do you suppose it is to no purpose that the Scripture says, "He yearns jealously over the spirit that he has made to dwell in us"? 6But he gives more grace. Therefore it says, "God opposes the proud, but gives grace to the humble." 7Submit yourselves therefore to God. Resist the devil, and he will flee from you. 8Draw near to God, and he will draw near to you. Cleanse your hands, you sinners, and purify your hearts, you double-minded. 9Be wretched and mourn and weep. Let your laughter be turned to mourning and your joy to gloom. 10Humble yourselves before the Lord, and he will exalt you.

Key Verse

Draw near to God, and he will draw near to you (James 4:8).

11Do not speak evil against one another, brothers. The one who speaks against a brother or judges his brother, speaks evil against the law and judges the law. But if you judge the law, you are not a doer of the law but a judge. 12There is only one lawgiver and judge, he who is able to save and to destroy. But who are you to judge your neighbor?

Go Deeper

People often react negatively to James's confrontational language, particularly his seemingly harsh words about friendship with the world. Truthfully, he doesn't pull any punches. "You adulterous people! Do you not know that friendship with the world is enmity with God? Therefore whoever wishes to be a friend of the world makes himself an enemy of God" (James 4:4).

Ouch! we think. But how does this affect any desire we might have to share the Gospel with people we know? Is witnessing a form of friendship with the world? Some of our confusion has to do with thinking that we can do whatever God does. So, we read in John 3:16 that "God so loved the world," and we conclude we should do the same. Then we read James 4:4 and 1 John 2:15—"Do not love the world." Here's the point. John 3:16 says that God loves all the people in the world. First John 2:15 cautions us not to love the way those people think, act and live. To be like God, we love people but not their sinful ways.

(continued)

Go Deeper Continued ...

One of the telltale signs of friendship with the world is fear of offense. If we don't talk about Jesus because we don't want to offend the world, we are directing our friendship in the wrong direction. Why would you hesitate to talk about your greatest friend, Jesus, who died for you? Show your love for people by not befriending those things they do that appall God. Instead, demonstrate the love of Christ in your witness to them.

There is probably no Bible writer that draws greater contrasts than James. His letter is filled with comparisons. He wants us to make wise choices, so he shows us the contrasts between such choices as resenting suffering or accepting suffering, having empty faith or exercising working faith, pursuing worldly wisdom or godly wisdom, and many more.

The choices we make have consequences. Bad choices lead to long-term bad consequences; good choices lead to good consequences. James presents a good choice: "Humble yourselves before the Lord" (James 4:10), and the consequence will be that "he will exalt you" (4:10). James 4:1–12 offers us a powerful contrast between friendship with the world and friendship with God.

It's worth remembering that James uses "you" thirteen times in the first five verses. The "you" he was addressing is the "brothers" of 3:12. James had Christians in mind. He doesn't ask *if* there are quarrels and fights; he asks his fellow believers if they understand what causes these divisions. When it comes to conflict in church, things haven't changed much since the first century. Instead of living as Jesus desired—"See how they love each other" (see John 13:35)—the world far too often looks at us and sees us behaving the same way they do! This is part of what James means by accusing his fellow believers (and us) of friendship with the world. Why should non-believers want to become believers if they can't see that it makes a difference in behavior?

In this chapter, James gives us six deliberate actions that will disarm quarrels and fights in the church and prevent us from being mistaken for the world. Action #1 is found in verse 7: "Submit yourselves therefore to God" (James 4:7). We can't have any doubts about our loyalty. We don't have to straighten out our lives and then submit to God—that's a task we can never accomplish without His help. We take the first, crucial action when we submit to Him, right where we are, in whatever mess we presently find ourselves.

After that, we can begin to take Action #2: "Resist the devil" (4:7). Satan desperately wants to convince us that he can still win, that he wasn't defeated at the cross. If he can convince us of his victory, he still won't win, but he will make us useless for the kingdom of God. We don't have to beat the devil; we only have to resist him. Defeating evil is such a daunting task that we often give up without any resistance! Resisting evil actually ought to appeal to our rebellious nature.

Action #3 states, "Draw near to God, and he will draw near to you" (v. 8). God leans out over the moral and spiritual canyon that separates us, longing for fellowship with us. But we can't reach or jump across the gap because our sin would immediately plunge us into the abyss. We can only draw near to God in the way He has graciously provided, through the blood of Jesus. We draw near by crossing the chasm on His cross.

Speaking of Jesus' unique role, the Book of Hebrews describes this process: "On the other hand, a better hope is introduced, through which we draw near to God" (Heb. 7:19). When we are drawing near to God, we will be less prone to friendship with the world.

Action #4 involves deliberate cleansing. "Cleanse your hands, you sinners, and purify your hearts, you double-minded" (James 4:8). Just as we can't "think or wish" our physical hands clean but must use soap and water, so our spiritual hands and heart need something beyond our desire in order to be clean.

"Satan desperately wants to convince us that he can still win, that he wasn't defeated at the cross. If he can convince us of his victory, he still won't win, but he will make us useless for the kingdom of God."

That something is the blood of Jesus Christ. His sacrifice created a fountain where we can be cleansed (see 1 John 1:9).

Action #5 will require humility, for we must "be wretched and mourn and weep" (James 4:9). These are outward signs of inward repentance. Our heartbroken awareness of sin may not take these exact forms, but if we are unwilling to show repentance, we are probably not willing to repent. We can certainly start with acknowledging our part in instigating and fostering quarrels and fights in the church. Admitting our involvement ought to bring about grief.

Action #6 arrives when we are ready to truly, "Humble [ourselves] before the Lord" (4:10). Bowing in humility before God is never out of style. The Bible urges us to develop genuine awe before the One who made us and loves us. (See Ps. 149:4; Prov. 3:34; Ezek. 21:26; Matt. 23:12; and 1 Pet. 5:6).

If we are busy taking these spiritual action steps, we won't have the time or the desire to participate in quarrels or fights among believers. And we might actually make an impact on the world because we're not trying so hard to imitate it.

Express It

Think for a few minutes about what it means to pray humbly. Would you say your usual way of approaching God is businesslike, casual or humble? What would it take for you to engage in a time of humble prayer, submitting yourself to God? Put the insights you receive into action.

Consider It

As you read James 4:1–12, consider these questions:

1) **What does James say are the causes for fights and quarrels among believers?**

The war of our passions within us.

2) **How do these root causes compare to the characteristics of earthly wisdom in James 3:14–15?**

They both are directly related to our own fleshly selfishness.

3) **How does friendship with the world affect our relationship with God?**

It takes us in the exact opposite direction; our worldly lusts & action make us enemies of God.

4) **When does God give us grace, and how much does He offer?**

God's amazing grace is always available to us (His sons) in its total abundance – always enough for what we need.

5) **How would you describe James's tone and approach in this passage?**

Very straight up, pulling no punches. He is very challenging & uses great leadership to direct us to God.

6) **Which of the corrective measures described in verses 7–10 do you find most helpful? Which is most difficult for you to do?**

v. 7 - submitting myself fully to Him first thing & quickly resisting the enemy.

7) **How do verses 11–12 keep us from applying these lessons to someone else rather than to ourselves?**

Is God in the Plan?

How long could you function without your calendar or PDA? Are you discovering your schedule is rapidly becoming the ultimate authority in your life? Have you had to start scheduling a few minutes each day when you "waste time, yawn and stop to smell the roses"? James puts our schedules and plans in perspective.

James 4:13–17

Boasting About Tomorrow

13Come now, you who say, "Today or tomorrow we will go into such and such a
town and spend a year there and trade and
make a profit"— 14yet you do not know
what tomorrow will bring. What is your life?
For you are a mist that appears for a little
time and then vanishes. 15Instead you
ought to say, "If the Lord wills, we will live
and do this or that." 16As it is, you boast in
your arrogance. All such boasting is evil.
17So whoever knows the right thing to do
and fails to do it, for him it is sin.

Key Verse

Instead you ought to say, "If the Lord wills, we will live and do this or that" (James 4:15).

Go Deeper

You've probably heard the sayings: "Failing to plan is like planning to fail," and "Aim at nothing and you'll hit it every time!" There's no doubt that God has designed life in such a way that planning is a good thing. It is good to identify a target before we shoot. It is an effective strategy to have a clear goal or purpose in mind before expending great amounts of effort. But there's a danger behind the fact that plans often succeed.

Plans that leave God out are not necessarily destined to fail. People unknowingly work out God's will all the time. The danger in a successful scheme has to do with pride. The greater the success, the greater grows the pride. And pride is the step just before the fall. (See Prov. 16:18.) History is littered with great successes followed almost immediately by destruction.

In the Bible, Daniel's account of the rise of Nebuchadnezzar offers a sobering example. Although he was warned about the danger of pride, he couldn't stop from boasting in his own glory: "Is not this great Babylon, which I have built by my mighty power as a royal residence and for the glory of my majesty?" (Dan. 4:30). The results of his arrogance (Dan. 4:1–37) remind us that one way or another, all of us will eventually be humbled before God (see Phil. 2:10–11).

Were James and his half-brother Jesus against planning? Did they live each day "shooting from the hip" without forethought or a schedule of any kind? When Jesus said, "Do not be anxious about tomorrow" (Matt. 6:34), did He mean, "Don't plan?" Absolutely not!

When Jesus talked about anxiety regarding tomorrow, He wasn't forbidding planning. In fact, planning is one of the best ways to deal with our tendency to worry about the future. We can't live in the future, but we can make wise plans for it. And the crucial part of a wise plan is including God before, during and after.

Jesus and James echo the ancient wisdom we find in places like Proverbs 16:9: "The heart of man plans his way, but the LORD establishes his steps." Proverbs 19:21 cautions, "Many are the plans in the mind of a man, but it is the purpose of the LORD that will stand."

James 4:12 ends with a question ("But who are you to judge your neighbor?") and 4:13 seems to begin a new subject. Most Bibles make that a paragraph break. The question may have been meant as rhetorical—one whose answer is obvious. But notice that 4:13 and 5:1 both begin with "Come now," an invitation to pay attention. James wants his readers to take these points personally. He is approaching the end of his letter with several biographical applications. He begins with a general appeal to people about the way they conduct their lives. Then he addresses the rich among the believers with scathing warnings. He follows this with the example of Job and Elijah as glowing models that we should follow. All of this encourages us to forget for a moment the failures of our neighbors and feel the full weight of God's truth on our lives.

James didn't accuse his readers of planning too much; he charged them with sloppy and careless planning. He pointed out they were planning like the world plans, making assumptions they wouldn't make if they included God in their plans. Sloppy planning takes the future for granted. It assumes we'll have not only tomorrow but next year and beyond (4:13). It assumes "profit" because to admit the possibility of loss would be to admit to limits on control. Careless planning doesn't take into account the brevity of life.

These mistakes shouldn't be used to argue against planning; instead they are excellent reasons for wise planning. People who won't accept how quickly life passes are people who aren't prepared for the sudden arrival of the future! These verses include three golden guidelines for Christians when they plan. They form this lesson's key verse: "Instead you ought to say, 'If the Lord wills, we will live and do this or that'" (v. 15).

Guideline #1—"If the Lord wills." This is the planning version of the prayer, "Your will be done." It is an admission that God gets the final say. We make plans but don't write them in stone. Our focus isn't on the shame of making the wrong plan but on the delight that God may have something even better in mind. We tend to think of God's will as limiting and disappointing. Why not think of it as liberating? There is great freedom in moving boldly with the confidence that God is in control even when things don't turn out as planned.

Guideline #2—"We will live." This is similar to the very healthy "'til death do us part" clause in the wedding vows. It's an acknowledgement of the daily "terminal possibilities" of life. It can be said of all people that life is not theirs. Life can come to an end at any moment. And believers in Jesus Christ should remember always that "you are not your own, for you were bought with a price. So glorify God in your body" (1 Cor. 6:19–20). There's a good dose of humility in remembering that we can't do the things we've planned if we're not here to do them.

Guideline #3—"Do this or that." If the first two guidelines are being followed, the specifics can be handled with flexibility. When the first two are ignored, we are left playing the role of

> *"We may not mean for our plans to sound arrogant, but if we ignore God in our plans, that's exactly what they are."*

being in control of our destiny. We may not mean for our plans to sound arrogant (James 4:16), but if we ignore God in our plans, that's exactly what they are. The world has the excuse that they don't know better. We don't have that excuse. We are left with James's words echoing in the depths of our souls: "So whoever knows the right thing to do and fails to do it, for him it is sin" (4:17). How many of your plans need to be revised to include God?

Express It

The difference between humility and arrogance can be seen in the way we plan and pray about the future. Do we trust God to provide the way, or are we insisting that our way is the only and best way? Spend some time praying about the way you plan and about the plans you have made. Spread them out before God, and acknowledge that you want His will to be done.

Consider It

As you read James 4:13–17, consider these questions:

1) **In what ways do you sense James's challenging your planning style in these verses?**

2) **What assumptions are made in the plan he describes in verse 13 about time, place and results?**

3) **How did James intend us to answer his question in verse 14: "What is your life?"**

4) **Describe in your words James's outline for planning from verse 15.**

5) **Referring to verse 16, is there any boasting that isn't evil? (See Jer. 9:23–24.)**

6) **How would you explain verse 17 to someone who is putting off or excusing himself or herself from a clear command of Scripture?**

7) **Use James's format to express several significant plans in your life.**

Lesson 9

Full Circle (Back to Patience)

Lack of patience leads to numerous problems in life—problems we create by trying to control life, and problems we create when our control fails. Most of us would rather have lives that didn't demand patience. But life, James shows us, is a multi-faceted training ground in patience.

James 5:1–12

Warning to the Rich

5 Come now, you rich, weep and howl for
the miseries that are coming upon you.
2Your riches have rotted and your garments
are moth-eaten. 3Your gold and silver have
corroded, and their corrosion will be evidence against you and will eat your flesh
like fire. You have laid up treasure in the
last days. 4Behold, the wages of the labor-
ers who mowed your fields, which you kept
back by fraud, are crying out against you,
and the cries of the harvesters have
reached the ears of the Lord of hosts. 5You
have lived on the earth in luxury and in
self-indulgence. You have fattened your
hearts in a day of slaughter. 6You have
condemned; you have murdered the righteous person. He does not resist you.

Patience in Suffering

7Be patient, therefore, brothers, until the
coming of the Lord. See how the farmer
waits for the precious fruit of the earth, being patient about it, until it receives the
early and the late rains. 8You also, be patient. Establish your hearts, for the coming
of the Lord is at hand. 9Do not grumble
against one another, brothers, so that you
may not be judged; behold, the Judge is
standing at the door. 10As an example of
suffering and patience, brothers, take the
prophets who spoke in the name of the
Lord. 11Behold, we consider those blessed
who remained steadfast. You have heard of
the steadfastness of Job, and you have
seen the purpose of the Lord, how the Lord
is compassionate and merciful.

> # *Key Verse*
>
> *You also, be patient. Establish your hearts, for the coming of the Lord is at hand* (James 5:8).

12But above all, my brothers, do not swear,
either by heaven or by earth or by any other oath, but let your "yes" be yes and your
"no" be no, so that you may not fall under
condemnation.

Go Deeper

The key verse (James 5:8) for this lesson includes an unusual phrase: "establish your hearts." Since this is a description of patience, it's worth unpacking. The language behind the phrase is sometimes translated "stand firm" or "strengthen your hearts." The expression can also be found in 1 Thessalonians 3:13 and 2 Thessalonians 2:17. Jesus didn't use these terms but captured the original thought when He said to His disciples, "Let not your hearts be troubled. Believe in God; believe also in me" (John 14:1). A heart that isn't established is a troubled heart.

The desperate measures taken by the rich in James 5:1–6 are evidence of the activities of a troubled heart. Jesus

(continued)

Go Deeper Continued ...

Himself described the effects created when treasures become the focus of our hearts: "For where your treasure is, there your heart will be also" (Matt. 6:21). An established heart is a heart resting on something that cannot be moved, shaken or changed. Matthew 7:24–27 describes the established heart as a house built on Jesus' words. In James 5:8 and John 14:1, the key to living with an untroubled, established heart is confidence in Christ's return or our departure to be with Him. Are you at peace with Jesus' possible return today?

James began his letter with an insight about patience in the face of trials. He ends his letter with the same theme. Much of the material within the letter has to do in part with the problems and struggles we have because we haven't learned to live by faith. But one of the shining characteristics of those who do live by faith is patience.

Although he included hints elsewhere (James 1:11–12; 2:1–8; 4:1–4,8–9) the first verses of James 5 give us the most bracing dose of confrontational words from this New Testament apostle. Years ago, an aftershave commercial pictured a man being slapped on both cheeks and then saying, "Thanks! I needed that!" Those willing to listen to the uncomfortable messages of the prophets throughout Scripture almost invariably have that response. The words feel like a slap, but we realize we needed to hear them.

James addressed the rich with uncompromising bluntness: "Come now, you rich, weep and howl for the miseries that are coming upon you" (5:1). The "miseries" may be what is in store for the rich, but they may also refer to the hard truths James is about to express. We can't be sure if James had the rich among Christians or the rich in general in mind, but if the descriptions fit, we ought to wear them.

The rich, James states, are people who tend to value perishable things (our earthly stuff) too highly while devaluing and defrauding eternal things (people). James's earlier comments on the rich had to do with a setting like a worship service. The setting has now shifted to the lifestyles of the wealthy, laying bare the underlying lack of integrity that invariably fills the lives of those who merely pursue the things of this world.

He lists six practices that build an overwhelming case against the rich. All of these can be seen as evidences of impatience—an unwillingness to live at God's pace and by God's values. First, the obvious "symbols of wealth" are subject to decay and destruction—they won't last (v. 2). The symbols of wealth may change throughout history, but they are all subject to the laws of a fallen world—they all wear out or rust out.

Second, even the most valued things like gold and silver can lose their value (v. 3), and we can't take them with us beyond the grave. James's words remind us of his brother's warning: "Do not lay up for yourselves treasures on earth, where moth and rust destroy and where thieves break in and steal" (Matt. 6:19). Hoarding with fear of the future or with thought only for this life is placing hope in what cannot sustain us.

Third, James points to those who have increased wealth by defrauding the ones who served them (James 5:4). God takes note of dishonesty and doesn't look kindly on it. Fourth, the rich have the means and the temptation to live "in luxury and in self-indulgence" (5:5). They recognize no need beyond their own. They don't see their God-given role in helping others. Fifth, despite evidences of coming judgment, the rich pursue habits that make them even more liable for judgment (v. 5). And sixth, the rich often have the power to rob others of their very lives by manipulating systems of government (v. 6).

Here James stops abruptly. If the cries of the defrauded reach the "ears of the Lord of hosts" (v. 4), surely the injustice done to those who have been condemned and murdered to insure the luxury of the rich will gain a hearing before God.

In contrast to the blatant impatience of the rich, James returns to his theme of patience. He includes at least six insights about patience in verses 7–12. 1) The spiritually patient are like farmers waiting for harvest (v. 7). 2) Patience requires an "established heart" (v. 8). 3) Patience requires a blameless attitude

"In order to 'be patient,' we must learn that God gives us new lessons in steadfastness every single day."

toward others (v. 9). 4) The patient gain encouragement and lessons from the saints of the past (v. 10). 5) Job serves as the patron saint of those in the school of patience (v. 11). 6) The patient speak the truth simply, without verbose impatience (v. 12). In order to "be patient," we must learn that God gives us new lessons in steadfastness every single day.

There are many striking similarities between the words of James and the words of Jesus. One can't help but wonder if even though he didn't believe in Jesus until after the Resurrection, James was deeply impressed by the profound wisdom in his half brother's teaching. Verse 12 almost quotes Jesus verbatim: "Let what you say be simply 'Yes' or 'No'; anything more than this comes from evil" (Matt. 5:37). In particular, James alludes to the lessons in the Sermon on the Mount (Matt. 5–7) more than any other book in the New Testament. He shows us the power in building our thoughts and vocabulary around the words of Jesus.

Express It

Review in prayer some of the circumstances God has used to build patience into your life. What patience-needing situations are you facing right now or are likely to face in the near future? Be thankful for God's past faithfulness, and express your desire to develop maximum patience from the lessons He provides.

Consider It

As you read James 5:1–12, consider these questions:

1) How do you react to the possibility of being numbered among the rich?

2) In what ways does James highlight the temptations you face with valuing things and devaluing people?

3) How does God want us to handle wealth?

4) What does patience have to do with the stewardship of wealth?

5) In what situations do believers tend to grumble against one another?

6) What kinds of examples can we get from the people in the Bible?

7) What is a significant lesson you've learned from this passage about developing patience?

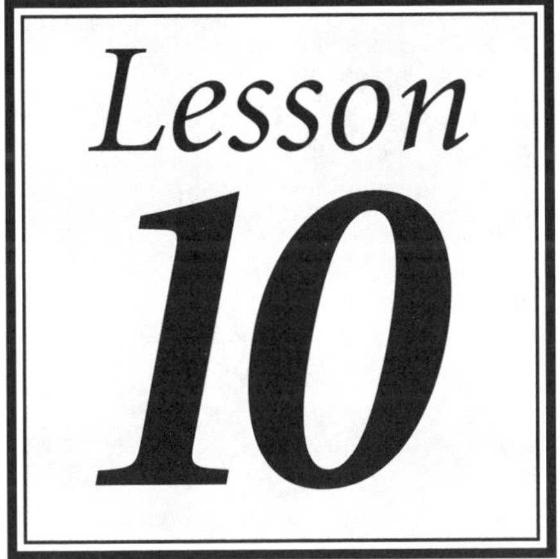

The Practicality of Prayer

Is prayer practical? When we pray, are we really accomplishing something or just passing the time? James strikes us as a man who was all about "doing." He didn't want us to avoid responsibilities. He encouraged us to have an active, living faith. So, what he says about prayer ought to be significant.

James 5:13–20

The Prayer of Faith

13Is anyone among you suffering? Let him
pray. Is anyone cheerful? Let him sing
praise. 14Is anyone among you sick? Let
him call for the elders of the church, and
let them pray over him, anointing him with
oil in the name of the Lord. 15And the
prayer of faith will save the one who is
sick, and the Lord will raise him up. And if
he has committed sins, he will be forgiven.
16Therefore, confess your sins to one another and pray for one another, that you
may be healed. The prayer of a righteous
person has great power as it is working.
17Elijah was a man with a nature like ours,
and he prayed fervently that it might not
rain, and for three years and six months it
did not rain on the earth. 18Then he prayed
again, and heaven gave rain, and the earth
bore its fruit.
19My brothers, if anyone among you wanders from the truth and someone brings
him back, 20let him know that whoever
brings back a sinner from his wandering
will save his soul from death and will cover
a multitude of sins.

Key Verse

Therefore, confess your sins to one another and pray for one another, that you may be healed. The prayer of a righteous person has great power as it is working (James 5:16).

Go Deeper

Coming from a no-nonsense, let's-get-busy-and-live-the-faith kind of person, James's closing thought in his letter catches us by surprise. His phrase, "if anyone among you wanders from the truth" (James 5:19), has a way of addressing each of us sooner or later.

Another reading of the last chapter shows us, moreover, that pastoral tenderness begins to take over from hard truth at about verse 7 with a heartfelt appeal to patience. Having preached patience, James closes his letter by practicing it.

It probably doesn't get pointed out often enough that when the apostle Paul wrote his great description of love in 1 Corinthians 13:4–8, the first trait he listed was patience. In order to carry out Jesus' command to love one another, you're going to have to start with a heavy dose of patience. What should be your motivation? It should be that others, including Christ, have been patient with you, and that others will need to be patient with you again! No one has been more patient with us, and therefore covered a multitude of sins, like Jesus Christ. Thank Him today.

James begins the closing section of his letter with an appeal to the practicality of prayer. He asks three pithy questions and offers essentially the same answer to each one. "Is anyone among you suffering? Let him pray. Is anyone cheerful?" (James 5:13), let him pray, too, since praise is one of the forms of prayer. And "is anyone among you sick?" (5:14). Get others to pray with you! Prayer was not an afterthought for James. It was forethought. The first question James asked in this letter (1:5) also received the same answer. "Do any of you lack wisdom?" Pray.

Over the last quarter century, the church seems to have developed a case of prayerlessness. We've emphasized worship, and we've become adept at corporate praise, but the prayer lives of some individual believers seem to be all but nonexistent. Prayer is not seen as practical. When we've tried everything else, then someone may suggest we pray. But prayer was not given to us as a last resort. It's often the most practical thing we do and sometimes the only really practical thing we can do. When was the last time someone asked you to pray for them or you asked them to pray for you, and you stopped right then and prayed together?

The success of a book like *The Prayer of Jabez* not long ago revealed a longing on the part of people to connect with God in ways that went beyond the "list of requests." People expressed a desire to see God involved in the day-to-day territory of life. In other words, people want to have a living faith that includes God in every part of life.

It was as if we woke up one day and realized that God existed for more than just the things that we couldn't handle. We had gotten used to thinking that the life of faith meant that we would take care of the little things like living, and He would be "there" for us when things got out of hand. Then, as someone wisely put it, we began to realize that there are no big things for God.

Everything is a little thing, and He wants us to trust Him with every little thing. As James noted, whether we're suffering, cheerful or sick, prayer should always be on our agenda.

James expected his readers would be involved in prayer on their own, as well as with each other. When he mentioned sickness, he also touched on a crucial issue in the life of faith—confession. Believers in that time were painfully aware of the connection between health and sin. This is not to say that illness is always or even usually the result of sin, but the fact is that sin and lack of confession can bring about sickness. Note that the prayer for a sick person (5:14–15) and his or her healing may involve forgiveness. This assumes that a compassionate prayer time for the sick person may include opportunity for the confession of sins.

Ultimately, as Jesus clearly illustrated in Mark 2:1–12, the deepest healing is forgiveness of sins. Though the man brought to the Lord had an obvious need to be healed of his paralysis, Jesus began with a more important issue—his need for forgiveness. Jesus' actions and words on that occasion announced to the world, "If My ability and willingness to heal people is a problem for you, you will never realize that I can and want to forgive sins!"

James's conclusion, "Therefore confess your sins to one another and pray for one another, that you may be healed" (James 5:16), was to encourage all of us. Spiritual health and restoration are connected with confession and relying on the prayers of others. Confession requires honesty, vulnerability and dependence on other believers. When we fail to be this open with each other, our prayers for each other will tend to be superficial and ineffective. And James wanted us to develop effective prayer lives. His mind turned to Elijah, the practitioner of meteorological prayer in the Old Testament. He held back the rains under God's command and then opened the spigot of heaven through prayer. James wanted us to have an enlarged view of prayer, not just so we could move mountains or seal up clouds, but so we could be confident of God's forgiveness, His answer to our prayer for deepest healing.

"There are no big things for God. Everything is a little thing, and He wants us to trust Him with every little thing."

The closing two verses in James's letter reveal the compassionate heart of a brother who resisted believing in Jesus for a long time. He wandered from the truth. But he was brought back when he discovered his half brother was indeed "the way, and the truth, and the life" (John 14:6). If it could happen for James, it could happen for any of us. That's the hopeful invitation of living faith.

Express It

This is an opportunity to pray about your prayer life. Based on this lesson's reading, are there some corrections that need to be made in the way you pray? Think about the people in your life for whom you could pray. What are their needs? How recently have you taken those needs to God? As you pray, ask God to put into your mind the names of two or three friends you could approach and offer to pray with them as a way of encouragement.

Consider It

As you read James 5:13–20, consider these questions:

1) **In what situations in life are you most likely to pray?**

2) **Based on this passage, why is prayer important?**

3) **What are some of the ways others can be involved in prayer for us?**

4) **Why should we confess our sins one to another?**

5) **How does James use Elijah as an example of prayer?**

6) **What situation is James describing in 5:19–20? In what ways are the roles of wanderer and "bringer back" familiar to you?**

7) **How would you describe the role of prayer in a life of faith?**

Living Your Faith

James's letter reads like a memo. It's a call to action. He challenges those who claim to have faith to demonstrate it by their lives. James was the original proponent of talk-the-talk and *walk-the-walk Christianity. The five chapters of James that we've just reviewed are some of the most compelling, convicting and motivating passages in Scripture.*

James 1:2–8; 2:14–26

Testing of Your Faith

2Count it all joy, my brothers, when you meet trials of various kinds, 3for you know that the testing of your faith produces steadfastness. 4And let steadfastness have its full effect, that you may be perfect and complete, lacking in nothing.

5If any of you lacks wisdom, let him ask God, who gives generously to all without reproach, and it will be given him. 6But let him ask in faith, with no doubting, for the one who doubts is like a wave of the sea that is driven and tossed by the wind. 7For that person must not suppose that he will receive anything from the Lord; 8he is a double-minded man, unstable in all his ways.

Key Verse

For you know that the testing of your faith produces steadfastness (James 1:3).

Faith Without Works Is Dead

14What good is it, my brothers, if someone says he has faith but does not have works? Can that faith save him? 15If a brother or sister is poorly clothed and lacking in daily food, 16and one of you says to them, "Go in peace, be warmed and filled," without giving them the things needed for the body, what good is that? 17So also faith by itself, if it does not have works, is dead.

18But someone will say, "You have faith and I have works." Show me your faith apart from your works, and I will show you my faith by my works. 19You believe that God is one; you do well. Even the demons believe—and shudder! 20Do you want to be shown, you foolish person, that faith apart from works is useless? 21Was not Abraham our father justified by works when he offered up his son Isaac on the altar? 22You see that faith was active along with his works, and faith was completed by his works; 23and the Scripture was fulfilled that says, "Abraham believed God, and it was counted to him as righteousness"—and he was called a friend of God. 24You see that a person is justified by works and not by faith alone. 25And in the same way was not also Rahab the prostitute justified by works when she received the messengers and sent them out by another way? 26For as the body apart from the spirit is dead, so also faith apart from works is dead.

Go Deeper

Bible students have long appreciated the parallels between the content of James's letter and Jesus' Sermon on the Mount. While the letter is fresh in your mind, take a few minutes to read through Jesus' message in Matthew 5–7. Note the similarities that stand out for you. In particular, how do Jesus' words about perse-

(continued)

Go Deeper Continued ...

cution (Matt. 5:10–12) match James's opening comments? Compare Jesus and James's comments on prayer (Matt. 7:7–11 and James 1:5; 5:15). How did both brothers handle direct questions? (See Matt. 5:33–37 and James 5:12.) How many more parallels can you find?

Both James and Jesus had things to say about humility (James 4:10; Matt. 5:3–4), and both practiced it. James certainly could have "pulled rank" in this letter and continually flaunted his special relationship with Jesus. There's no hint of that. James simply echoed his big brother's teaching and let the truth speak for itself. This is another example of James's central point that we validate the truth and depth of what we have learned not just by what we say but by the way we live out our faith.

You can read through James's letter in about half an hour. But it takes a lifetime to live the principles he wrote about. Clearly, Jesus' half brother was a committed follower who took to heart Jesus' words spoken shortly before going to the cross: "Whoever has my commandments and keeps them, he it is who loves me" (John 14:21).

We who are accustomed to thinking about love and faith in terms of feelings and ideas can easily find ourselves "putting on the brakes" as we read James's letter. But the problem isn't that James is so much more practical than the other writers of the New Testament; the problem is that we misread the rest of the New Testament as ideas rather than life-changing action. In every place that God's Word speaks to us about faith, it is speaking to us about a living, everyday and everywhere kind of faith.

James would probably have said a hearty "amen" to the brief directions Saint Francis of Assisi gave to his traveling preachers. "Go everywhere and share the Gospel. If necessary, use words!" The truth is, the world is often unwilling to listen to the Gospel we have to share because they have been watching us, and they don't like what they see. Talking can prepare for doing, encourage doing and explain doing, but talking is not an effective substitute for doing.

While living in New England during my college, seminary and early pastoral days, I came to know that the culture in that part of the United States illustrates the point James makes repeatedly in his letter. A story is told about a man on a trip who decided to take a few days of relaxation in New England. He stopped in a small town and checked into the old hotel on the square. As he carried his bags into the hotel, he noticed the wide porch, occupied by several men in rocking chairs. They seemed to be enjoying the cool summer evening. He said, "Hello." They nodded.

After he was settled in his room, the man decided to join the guys on the porch. He sat in one of the empty rocking chairs and joined the soft chorus of creaks as they rocked. After a few moments of silence, the man commented, "Nice weather we're having."

There was no response from the others. The rocking continued. Puzzled, the man tried another conversation starter, "Must be nice to enjoy the quiet evenings around here." Again, no response from his companions. After a couple of other attempts at instigating talk, the man grabbed the chair next to his and looked the occupant in the eyes. He said, "Is there a law against talking in this town?"

An old New Englander looked calmly back at him and said, "Nope. Ain't no law. Just want to make sure what we say is an improvement on silence."

Every chapter in James has at least one example of speaking that isn't an improvement on silence (1:13; 2:3,16; 3:10,14; 4:3,11; 5:9,12). Like the New Englanders, James wanted us to think twice before we speak. Cleary, James wasn't against verbal communication—after all, he did write a letter! But he was cautious of the way our tongues get us into trouble. None of us completely avoids verbal stumbles (James 3:2), but the best way to prevent stumbles from becoming disasters is to live a life that shows the stumble as an exception rather than a rule. If our verbal stumbles simply echo our lives, we make little progress in representing Jesus Christ in the world.

"The world is often unwilling to listen to the Gospel we have to share because they have been watching us, and they don't like what they see. Talking can prepare for doing, encourage doing and explain doing, but talking is not an effective substitute for doing."

Any believer who longs to live for Christ in the world can benefit from continued study of the letter of James. The letter will provide plenty to keep you busy living your faith and will step in to humble your pride anytime you are taking credit for your successes. And don't forget James's final lesson. He lived half a lifetime with his big brother Jesus, unable to recognize Him as the Son of God. Jesus was patient with James; that little brother never forgot that. Paul tells us that Jesus paid His half-brother a special visit after the Resurrection. (See 1 Cor. 15:7.) It was time to leave doubt and familiarity behind and live by faith. James did just that. You can too.

Express It

Hopefully this study, like James's letter, will begin and end with prayer. He first called you to pray for wisdom (James 1:5) and then eventually urged you to ask others to pray for you and then for you to pray for them. Practice that right now. Talking to God can be an improvement on silence as long as we save enough silence in prayer to also listen to what God may have to say to us.

Consider It

As you read James 1:2–8 and 2:14–26, consider these questions:

1) **What lasting impact has this study of James made on your life?**

2) **What changes are you considering as a result of this study?**

3) **How would you summarize James's central message?**

4) **In what ways does silence fit into living out your faith?**

5) **How do you decide when you have something to say that's an improvement on silence?**

6) **What's a question you would like to ask Jesus' younger brother?**

Notes

Notes

Notes

Notes

Notes

Notes